From Carbon Copies to Cloud Co

# A Note to the Newer L

*(or anyone who's ever Googled "*

Hey there,

If you're wondering what "Carbon Copies" are or why they're in the title, don't worry, you don't need to know to understand this book. This isn't a trip down memory lane just for nostalgia's sake.

This is a collection of real, raw, sometimes ridiculous stories from my 32+ years in real estate, each one tied to a lesson I *promise* you'll use. I've been a licensee, a broker, a trainer, a fixer, a mentor, and sometimes the one running from exploding cans of baked beans (true story, you'll see).

The tools we use have changed - from ink and pen to digital signatures, from expensive magazine ads to online leads & social media marketing, from rooms full of file cabinets to cloud storage that will fit on a flash drive small enough to stash in a pocket. Our industry has changed into a virtual toolbox, but the core of our business hasn't. People. Problems. Risk. Trust. Judgment. Mistakes. Recovery.

That's the stuff that makes or breaks a career.

So if you're newer to this industry, I wrote this for *you*. If I can save you from one bad showing, one lawsuit, or one terrible dishwasher mistake, this book has done its job.

You don't have to learn everything the hard way.

But I sure did, so you don't have to.

TjB

For Will:

When I was young, unsure, and about to step into an industry I knew nothing about, you didn't hesitate. I told you I wanted to try real estate, that it would cost money we didn't really have for classes, licensing, dues, and that I'd basically be working for free until I could earn a commission. You didn't flinch.

You said, *"You can do anything you want. I support your decision, and we'll figure it out."* That moment changed everything. Thank you for believing in me when I didn't yet believe in myself.

For Travis and Scooter:

You boys were my security team before I even knew I needed one, going on appointments with me, helping with showings and cleanups. Thank you for being my plus-one at more banquets and ceremonies than you ever asked for. And Scooter, for being part of the story that became *Beans, Burn Barrels & Barney*. Travis, for marrying Jessica, my first real assistant, and supporting both of us in more ways than I could ever explain.

This book is as much yours as it is mine.

Harley & Marlys Tessier

Before I ever stepped into a real estate office, Will and I were in a terrible accident. I suffered a traumatic brain injury that left me battling debilitating headaches and seizures. I wasn't able to drive for nearly a year.

My parents, Harley and Marlys, had moved back to Alaska to be close to me and help out. They were there in the ways that truly matter. One day, my dad asked if I'd consider getting into real estate with him. I told him, *"No, Dad. I'm not a salesperson."* And I'll never forget what he said next, something I've shared with countless licensees and students ever since:

"We aren't salespeople. We are providing professional service to people who have already made a decision they are going to buy or sell real estate."

That one sentence reframed everything. He wasn't in the business long, but his perspective stayed with me, and it's guided the way I've done business ever since.

And my mom? She was right there, always supportive. I often joke with new licensees, *"When I started in real estate, my mommy had to drive me to showing appointments."* But it's more than a joke, it's a truth. She was my driver, my cheerleader, and my steady voice.

They've both passed on now, but their legacy lives on. Before they left this world, I named my LLC after them, Marley T Group LLC, a blend of their names: *Marlys & Harley Tessier*. Because every success I've had started with the foundation they gave me.

※

# Preface:

Real estate has changed dramatically over the past three decades, from carbon copy contracts and fax machines to cloud-based systems and e-signatures. But what hasn't changed is the human element at the heart of every transaction: the people we serve, the challenges we navigate, and the hard-won lessons we gather along the way.

I'm Traci J. Barickman, and after more than 32 years as a real estate broker, educator, and mentor in Alaska, I've seen it all, laugh-out-loud moments, cringe-worthy rookie mistakes (some of them mine), and countless reminders of why safety, ethics, and good instincts matter. I've supervised thousands of transactions, supported hundreds of licensees, and found myself in more than one situation where the only way out was quick thinking, a sense of humor, and solid documentation.

*From Carbon Copies to Sign & Send* isn't just a memoir or a manual, it's a conversation. It's my way of passing down stories that are too valuable (and sometimes entertaining) to keep to myself, paired with practical takeaways that just might save your next deal, or your career.

Whether you're a brand-new licensee, a seasoned professional, or someone who just enjoys a good story, I hope this book brings you insight, encouragement, and a few well-earned laughs.

# Introduction: Why I Wrote This Book

Constant reflection. I've spent more than three decades in this industry and as a result, I'm always thinking. Thinking about what just happened. Thinking about what's happening now. Thinking about what's coming next. What I should've done. What I could've done. Whether I handled that last situation the way I *meant* to, or whether I could have done better.

That constant reflection is what shaped this book.

These stories are pulled from real life; mine, my licensees', and the world we all navigate as professionals who carry other people's dreams on our shoulders. They're unfiltered, honest, and sometimes a little messy. Because that's what real estate is: a job that lives at the intersection of logic and emotion, pressure and personality.

If you're reading this, you're likely someone I've worked with, past or present, or someone walking a path like mine. This book is for you. It's a collection of teachable moments wrapped in laughter, chaos, hard lessons, and the kind of wisdom you only get by *living it*.

And maybe, in some small way, this is also my prelude to the exit. Not a goodbye, but a passing of the torch. A chance to say: I've been there. I've made the mistakes. I've seen what happens when we cut corners and when we show up.

If these stories help you pause, adjust course, or feel a little more seen in this unpredictable business, then this book has done its job.

෴

# Table of Contents

Preface
Introduction: Why I Wrote This Book

Chapter One: Danger Doesn't Always Knock
  - Basements, Padlocks & Bad Decisions
  - The Hallway That Changed My Safety Protocols
  - The Mold House
  - One Wrong Reach
  - Reflection & Discussion

Chapter Two: Paper Trails & Pitfalls
  - Drawing Inside the Lines
  - The Power of Documentation
  - Reflection & Discussion

Chapter Three: Contracts, Chaos & Closing Day Curveballs
  - The Costly Oversight
  - The 58-Foot Mistake
  - The Grow Operation
  - Reflection & Discussion

Chapter Four: Service, Standards & Showing Up
  - Signed But Not Delivered
  - Thanksgiving Regret
  - Ethical Dilemma
  - Reflection & Discussion

Chapter Five: Barney's Wrap-Up
  - Beans, Burn Barrels & Barney

Acknowledgments

# Chapter 1: Danger Doesn't Always Knock

## *Safety Isn't Rude, It's Smart*

Early in my career, I thought being accommodating was part of the job. Smile, nod, open the door, let people lead the way. I didn't want to seem overly cautious or make anyone uncomfortable. But real estate can take you into remote cabins, bank-owned properties, and basements that haven't seen light in decades. And while most days are perfectly ordinary, it only takes *one* to remind you that safety isn't optional, it's essential.

This section shares some of the moments that changed how I view safety, not just physical safety, but environmental awareness and the importance of *pausing before you proceed*. These stories aren't meant to scare you; they're here to make you think. Because when you're out there doing the job, there's no rewind button.

If you remember nothing else, remember this: Being safe isn't being rude; it's being smart. And smart keeps you alive.

# Basements, Padlocks, & Bad Decisions

In the early years of my real estate career, before cell phones were common and when we still relied on printed maps and gut instincts, I scheduled a listing appointment at the home of a couple I had never met. It was in a fairly remote part of town, but that wasn't unusual. What was unusual, in hindsight, was how casual (clueless) I was about the safety protocols I *should* have had in place.

When I arrived at the property, the man greeted me at the door and invited me inside. He seemed friendly enough, but a little 'off'. The home wasn't well kept, the neighborhood not the safest. The man proceeded to show me around the home. As we made our way from room to room, I was asking questions and keeping notes, but feeling increasingly uncomfortable, and I didn't know why.

Then he offered to show me the basement. Without thinking twice, I agreed, and here's where the first mistake happened. I went down the stairs *ahead* of him, letting him position himself between me and the only exit. Rookie mistake.

Once in the basement, I scanned the space. Across the far wall, he motioned to a small mechanical room and said, "Let me show you this." I walked toward it, only to realize as I got closer that the door had a *padlock on the outside*. It was clearly designed to lock someone *in*. That's when my gut finally kicked in. My mind raced through every scenario I'd ever seen on a crime show, and I made a quick decision to casually back away, make a polite excuse, and head back up the stairs slowly, without showing panic. Fortunately, he didn't try to stop me.

I got out of that house safely, but I've thought about that moment more times than I can count. It was the first major wake-up call of my career.

☙

## Key Takeaways:

- Never allow someone to get between you and the exit: Whether you're meeting a new client or showing a property for the first time, always maintain an escape route. Positioning matters.

- Listen to your gut: If something feels off, even slightly, pause and assess. Trust your instincts.

- Don't let familiarity breed carelessness: The longer you're in real estate, the easier it becomes to skip protocols. Don't. Risk doesn't decrease with experience; sometimes, it increases with complacency.

- Bring a safety buddy or check-in system: Especially for appointments in rural areas, vacant properties, or with new contacts, tell someone where you're going and when you expect to be back.

Notes: _____

_____
_____
_____
_____
_____
_____
_____
_____
_____
_____
_____
_____
_____
_____
_____
_____

# The Hallway that Changed my Safety Protocols

Years later, with more experience under my belt, but still more to learn, I was showing a newly constructed home in Anchorage. It was a large two-story property built on top of a full-sized garage. I had left the key in the front door lock, something I often did in the quieter areas of the Valley where I felt more secure. That was mistake number one. The buyers were a married couple, but only the wife could attend the showing in person. I spoke with her husband on the phone during the tour to include him in the showing.

It was a typical showing, until it wasn't.

We made our way to the top floor, exploring the spacious master suite at the end of a long hallway.

While still chatting with the husband on the phone, I heard a noise downstairs. I dismissed it as the builder coming in, after all, the house wasn't quite finished, and contractors often popped in. That was mistake number two.

A few minutes later, while showing the wife the master bathroom, I heard someone coming up the stares at the end of the hallway, so I glanced down the hallway and saw a man standing at the far end, staring at me. He looked *angry*. He wasn't the builder. He didn't knock. He didn't announce himself. He just appeared.

He started down the hall toward me.

I fought panic and instinct took over. Here is where I almost made mistake #3. I started to tell the husband I needed to hang up, but then realized he may be our lifeline, so I handed the phone to the wife and quietly told her, "Go into the bathroom, lock the door, and keep your husband on the line."

The man stormed down the hallway, confronted me, and started yelling at me; he was angry about the construction, about the noise, about the constant traffic. He was a neighbor, not the builder. And he was furious. And he was taking his frustrations out on me, thinking I was representing the builder.

Thankfully, it was just a confrontation. I was able to de-escalate the situation by speaking calmly to him and explaining my position. This incident taught me something crucial: Don't make assumptions, situational awareness is crucial at all times. Always have a lifeline. And never, ever leave the key in the door.

ॐ

## Key Takeaways:

- Always Maintain Situational Awareness: Just because a property is vacant or under construction doesn't mean you're alone. Assume someone could walk in at any moment, because they can.

- Never Assume You Know Who's Entering the Property: That sound downstairs? It might be the builder, but it might not. Always verify and prepare accordingly.

- Don't Leave the Key in the Door: It might be convenient, but it's a major safety risk. You're inviting unannounced visitors, whether it's a neighbor, contractor, or someone with bad intentions.

- Have a Lifeline: The instinct to hang up the phone could have left both me and my client vulnerable. Keeping someone on the line can be critical in escalating situations. It can serve as both witness and support.

- Protect Your Clients: It's your job to keep them safe, too. Directing the wife to a secure location and ensuring communication was maintained was the right call. In high-stress moments, quick thinking and clear direction matter.

- Calm De-escalation Can Save the Day: Even in tense confrontations, staying calm and respectful can diffuse a volatile situation. Match emotion with steady presence, not more emotion.

# Don't Forget to Look Up

*When the real danger is the one you can't see, or smell, until it's too late.*

There are some things you never forget, the texture of shag carpet soaked in cat urine, the scent of mildew in a crawlspace, the weird, unsettling hum of an empty house that's been closed up too long.

But nothing prepared me for this one.

Years ago, I was working with a builder client who had his eye on a remote piece of property with a rustic, decades-old cabin. It had been vacant for a while, and from the outside, it looked like the kind of place you'd expect to see in an old Alaska homesteading photo, weathered wood, sagging porch, that sort of charm.

We stepped inside, the air stale and thick with that "abandoned building" smell. Dust coated everything, but the structure was sound. There was a built-in ladder leading to a loft, and being the ever-curious professional I was, I climbed right up to check it out.

About halfway up, I could already sense something wasn't quite right. But when I reached the top and poked my head into the loft, there it was, a massive, black, glistening BLOB. It didn't move. It just… sat there. Rank. Lumpy. Ominous.

I froze. "What the heck is that?" I asked.

My builder, still standing below, calmly said: "Look up."

So, I did.

The entire ceiling above the loft was alive, black and writhing. Bats. A colony of them.

Apparently, the blob was, well, let's just say it was WHAT'S LEFT BEHIND after bats have made themselves at home for a long time.

# Key Takeaways: When Vacant Isn't Vacant

- **Vacant doesn't mean empty** – Always be cautious when entering older, unoccupied structures.

- **Look, listen, and sniff** – Your senses can often tell you more than a listing description ever will.

- **Health hazards are real** – Bat guano (yes, that's what it was) can carry histoplasmosis, a serious lung infection. Be mindful of what you're breathing in.

- **Even seasoned professionals can be caught off guard** – Curiosity is part of the job, but so is caution.

Notes: _____
_____
_____
_____
_____
_____
_____
_____
_____
_____
_____
_____
_____
_____
_____
_____
_____
_____
_____
_____
_____
_____
_____

# The Mold House

There's a certain kind of stillness in abandoned properties. No electricity humming, no air movement, no voices. Just silence. And sometimes, that silence feels like a warning.

It was a bank-owned mobile home, long vacant. The bank had asked me to preview the property and report back with a valuation and condition notes, nothing unusual. I pulled up, unlocked the door, and stepped inside.

Immediately, I felt it, nausea. My stomach turned the moment the door closed behind me. But I was young, new to real estate, and still thought being thorough meant pushing through discomfort. So I stayed.

That was mistake number one.

I walked into the kitchen, and it hit me. Every surface, every cabinet, every wall, every bit of countertop, was coated in thick, black mold. Not the kind you get from a leaky sink. This was the full horror movie treatment. Spores in the air. Spores on the walls. Spores probably in my lungs.

But I kept going. That was mistake number two.

In my inexperience, I thought, "Well, I'm already here,I might as well finish the walkthrough."

I can look back now and say it was foolish. Mold like that isn't just unsightly, it's *dangerous*. I didn't know it at the time, but exposure to high levels of black mold spores can cause serious respiratory problems, immune system suppression, and long-term health issues. I had no mask, no gloves, no eye protection. Nothing.

I just didn't know better.

Now, I do. And so do the licensees I train. Because this is one of those lessons you only need to learn *once*.

☙

## Key Takeaways:

- Trust your instincts – If something feels off when you enter a property, listen to that inner alarm. Your body might be picking up on environmental danger before your brain catches up.
- Mold is more than cosmetic – Prolonged exposure to black mold can have serious health consequences. It isn't just "gross," it's hazardous.
- Leave when it's unsafe – Don't risk your health for a preview, a showing, or a valuation. If a space feels compromised, walk out and reschedule with proper safety gear.
- Bring basic PPE – Keep a kit in your car: N95 mask, gloves, booties, flashlight. You never know what you'll walk into.
- Early-career overconfidence is real – Sometimes our biggest risks come from simply not knowing what we don't know. Share your missteps so others can avoid repeating them.

NOTES:_____

_____
_____
_____
_____
_____
_____
_____
_____
_____
_____
_____
_____
_____
_____
_____

# One Wrong Reach

One of my licensees shared this story with me a few years ago, and I've thought about it often since.

A buyer's licensee was showing a property, casually walking through with his client, both of them chatting as they went. They approached the man-door to the garage, still deep in conversation. Without missing a beat, the licensee opened the door and reached instinctively into the darkness for a light switch, something we've all done a hundred times.

But this time, what he reached into wasn't a switch.

It was an exposed electrical panel.

In a fraction of a second, everything changed. He suffered severe burns, the kind that require immediate medical attention and leave permanent reminders. The panel had no cover. No warning. Just live wires sitting in the shadows, waiting for a hand that didn't look first.

When the story was relayed to me, it hit hard. Because I've done the exact same thing, many times. Many of us have. We assume we know the layout. We move on autopilot. We trust that if there's danger, it'll be labeled, obvious, or at least out of reach.

But sometimes, danger is right where your hand goes first.

Since hearing that story, I've made it a rule: Stop. Look. Then reach. Always.

Key Takeaways:

- Slow down and look. Even familiar spaces deserve a second of caution. Assumptions are where most injuries begin.
- Never reach into darkness. Bring a flashlight or use your phone's light before entering dark garages, crawlspaces, or sheds.
- What we model, others mimic. Clients (especially buyers) watch how we move through spaces. Be the example.
- Tell these stories. Sometimes the best way to protect someone is by sharing the pain someone else endured.

Notes: _____

_____
_____
_____
_____
_____
_____
_____
_____
_____
_____
_____
_____
_____
_____
_____
_____
_____
_____
_____
_____

# Chapter Wrap-Up: What We Don't See Can Hurt Us

It's easy to picture physical danger in this job as something visible, a suspicious person, a broken stair tread, or a padlocked room in a basement. But not all threats walk on two legs. Some grow quietly in the dark, or flap above your head, unnoticed until it's too late.

Environmental hazards like mold, infestations, or even air quality issues are every bit as serious as client safety concerns. Just like the bat-infested loft I climbed into years ago, the black mold house reminded me that danger doesn't always knock, it sometimes just waits.

What these stories have in common is simple: Don't ignore discomfort. Don't hesitate to leave. And don't let pride or politeness override your safety instincts. Whether it's airborne toxins or a ceiling full of bats, if something feels off, it probably is.

## Reflection & Discussion

1. Have you ever felt uncomfortable or unsafe during a showing or appointment?
   What did you do , and what do you wish you had done differently?

2. How has your mindset around safety evolved since you first started in real estate?
   Are there habits or precautions you take now that you didn't used to?

3. Think about the places or types of properties that present the biggest risks.
   How can you prepare for or avoid those risks while still doing your job effectively?

4. When was the last time you prioritized being "nice" over being smart?
   What stops us from setting boundaries , and how can we shift that?

5. What do you model for new licensees, assistants, or clients when it comes to safety?
   What message are they picking up from the way you handle uncertain situations?

# Chapter Two

## Paper Trails & Pitfalls

*Intro: The Details Always Matter*

In real estate, it's not the big stuff that usually gets you , it's the details you *thought* someone else was handling. The missing addendum. The assumption that a survey was accurate. The "I'm sure the buyer understood that" moment that ends up in litigation six months later.

We all want to believe that good intentions are enough, but in this business, what's written down is what counts. Documentation isn't just about CYA , it's about protecting your clients, protecting yourself, and making sure everyone knows what was agreed to, when, and why.

This section dives into the critical (and often overlooked) power of paper trails. These stories remind us how easy it is to miss a detail , and how important it is to slow down, double-check, and never assume.

Because if it's not documented, it didn't happen.

# The Power of Documentation

Some lessons in real estate don't come from mistakes you make, but from the ones you AVOID by doing things right.

Years ago, I was representing a seller on an 8-acre parcel with highway frontage. The lot had potential, and while it seemed ideal for commercial development, I wasn't certain of its zoning or permitted uses, so I made a deliberate decision: I didn't advertise it as commercial. That was the first safeguard. I was new, and didn't even know how to research it.

One day, I got a call from a builder. He was experienced, successful, and came without a buyer's licensee. He wanted to write the offer directly with me. I gave my standard disclosure about representation and my role in the transaction. Then I handed him everything I had, title, plat, covenants, restrictions, and property disclosures.

The deal moved along smoothly and closed without a hitch. Fast forward about six months, and the phone rang. It was him.

He was frustrated, actually, he was upset. Turns out, he had planned to build a commercial structure on the parcel and had just found out that the property could only be used for residential or recreational purposes. "Why didn't you tell me?" he demanded.

But here's the thing: I HAD (ALBEIT UNKNOWINGLY) told him. In fact, I had him sign and acknowledge receipt of every single document, including the full set of CCRs (Covenants, Conditions & Restrictions). I kept copies, and I kept notes. In those early days of paper files and three-ring binders, I had the entire transaction printed and organized. I pulled it out, flipped to the CCRs, and there it was: his initials on every page, and his signature on the acknowledgment form.

I sent him the documents, and the conversation ended right there. No attorney, no threats, no damage control. Just a phone call… and a paper trail.

Key Takeaways:

- **Document Everything.** Verbal conversations are great, but if it's not in writing, it didn't happen. Keep detailed notes and follow up any important conversation with written confirmation.

- **Get Acknowledgments.** Make sure your buyers and sellers sign for every document, especially anything relating to property use, CCRs, or disclosures. Their signature is your shield.

- **Protect Yourself, Even from Experienced Clients.** Don't assume that seasoned buyers read everything. Hand it to them. Point it out. Make sure they know what they're signing.

- **Good Files Save You.** Whether it's digital or old-school paper, an organized file can mean the difference between a closed case and a legal headache.

- **Don't Oversell.** If you're unsure of a property's zoning or usage potential, don't market it as something it might not be. Let the documentation speak.

Notes: _____

_____
_____
_____
_____
_____
_____
_____
_____
_____
_____
_____
_____

# Drawing Inside the Lines

I was a few years into my career as a broker when one of my licensees came to me in a bit of a panic. She was representing a seller client; someone she had helped buy the same home a few years earlier when it was newly constructed. Now, that same home was back on the market, but a hidden issue had surfaced.

Back when her client purchased the property, the builder had provided an as-built survey, a standard request to confirm the home and improvements were correctly placed within the lot boundaries. The survey showed no red flags. Everything looked clean. The sale closed, and life moved on.

Now that the client was selling, the new buyer's licensee insisted on ordering a fresh as-built survey. At first, my licensee questioned the need, nothing had changed on the property. But the buyer pushed, and thankfully, they followed through.

The new survey came back, and it showed something the original didn't: an encroachment into the setback easement for a section line. The house had been built too close to the boundary. Confused, the licensee compared the new as-built to the original, only to discover that the original had been altered. Someone had used white-out to erase the section line easement on the paper survey. That "someone" turned out to be the builder.

It was a clear case of fraud, and had the buyer not insisted on a new as-built, they would've inherited the problem, and possibly passed it on to the next buyer, making their own licensee liable in the future.

This was a powerful reminder that even when everything LOOKS fine, due diligence is never optional. That small decision to update a survey prevented a legal nightmare and protected not only the buyer but also the professionals involved.

Key Takeaways:

- **Always recommend updated surveys**, even if "nothing has changed." A fresh asbuilt can reveal issues that weren't visible before or were deliberately hidden.

- **Trust but verify.** Just because something looks official doesn't mean it hasn't been tampered with.

- **Document everything.** A clean paper trail could be the difference between a smooth transaction and a lawsuit.

- **Advocate for your clients, even when it feels redundant.** Good representation sometimes means asking the hard questions or requesting things twice.

- **Protect your future self.** When you're thorough today, you avoid liability tomorrow.

Notes: _____

_____
_____
_____
_____
_____
_____
_____
_____
_____
_____
_____
_____
_____
_____

# Reflection & Discussion

1. Have you ever been saved (or burned) by documentation? What happened, and how did it shape your process moving forward?

2. How do you ensure your contracts, disclosures, and files are consistently clean and complete?
What's your personal system, and is it working?

3. What's your process for verifying things like surveys, maps, or seller disclosures?
Do you ever assume someone else has it handled?

4. Have you ever experienced a moment where a lack of documentation cost someone - you, your client, or another licensee, time, money, or trust?

5. What habits would you teach a new licensee about tracking communication, verifying details, or documenting decisions?

Notes: _____

_____
_____
_____
_____
_____
_____
_____
_____
_____
_____
_____
_____
_____
_____
_____
_____

# Chapter Three

## Contracts, Chaos & Closing Day Curveballs

*You Can't Fix What You Didn't Catch*

Every transaction looks clean on paper until it isn't. One missed checkbox, one outdated plat or as-built, one buyer who *didn't really read* the contract, and suddenly you're managing damage control instead of a smooth close.

Contracts are the backbone of what we do, but they're only as strong as the people filling them out. This section covers the moments where things got messy, not because someone was malicious, but because someone wasn't paying attention. Sometimes it was a licensee. Sometimes it was a builder. And sometimes, it was just a perfect storm of timing, trust, and poor communication.

The lessons? Check everything. Ask the uncomfortable questions. And don't ever assume the other side, or your transaction coordinator, is catching the stuff you're too tired to read.

Because when it comes to contracts, "close enough" is never close enough.

## The Costly Oversight

This story is about the importance of paying attention to detail and truly understanding your contracts and financial allocations when representing clients.

One of my new licensees wrote an offer on behalf of his buyer for a property listed by a seasoned, top-producing licensee at another brokerage. In the additional terms and conditions of the offer, he asked the seller to cover the buyer's closing costs , and it was a substantial amount. When completing the purchase agreement, he allocated the majority of the closing costs to the seller's side , including those that are typically split or buyer-paid.

The listing licensee, though highly experienced and very busy, was complacent in her review of the offer. She presented it to the seller without calling attention to the full financial impact. The seller agreed and signed, unaware they were committing to pay not only their own closing costs, but the entire amount for the buyer as well.

It wasn't until the final settlement statement was issued that the magnitude of the oversight became clear. The buyer was thrilled , he felt like his licensee had pulled off a brilliant deal. But the seller? Not so much. He was blindsided and extremely unhappy with his own representation. Understandably, he felt let down by the licensee he trusted to protect his interests.

&♥

## Key Takeaways:

- Experience doesn't excuse inattention. Even top-producing licensees can make critical errors when they become complacent.

- Review every line. Proper allocation of closing costs requires a careful review of the contract, even if the amounts look standard.

- Represent both sides fairly. If you're the listing agent, it's your job to help your client understand what they're agreeing to.

- Communication is key. Mistakes often slip through when people are rushed, distracted, or overly trusting of the process.

- Clients deserve vigilance. Your value as a licensee lies not just in writing offers, but in protecting your clients through precision and professionalism.

Notes: _____

_____
_____
_____
_____
_____
_____
_____
_____
_____
_____
_____
_____
_____
_____
_____
_____

# The 58-Foot Mistake

Early in my career, I sold a property that already had a driveway, well, septic, and a building foundation in place. My buyer planned to build a home for his family right on that foundation. We were aware there was a section line easement on the property, so we requested a survey to mark the boundaries. The survey confirmed that the foundation was about 20 feet inside the property line. Confident in the survey results, we closed the deal, and construction began.

What I didn't know at the time, and what no one had taught me, was that section line easements in our area typically come with a 33-foot easement and a 25-foot setback requirement. That meant no permanent structures could be built within 58 feet of the section line. Unfortunately, the foundation encroached on that space by roughly 38 feet.

It was a major issue, and I had no guidance from my broker or office. So, I did what I've always done when faced with a challenge: I dove in and started learning. I researched variances, zoning ordinances, and potential exceptions. I discovered that in some cases, it might be possible to vacate the section line easement if it could be proven unnecessary for public use.

That turned out to be a big "if."

The section line in question passed through several private parcels, but a few lots down, it terminated at a river. And as I learned, the State does not easily give up public access to bodies of water , unless there's an alternate route that provides equal or better access.

It took me 18 months, countless hours, and multiple visits to local, state, and federal agencies, but eventually, I succeeded in getting that portion of the easement vacated. My client was able to keep his foundation and move forward with building his family's home , and I walked away with one of the most valuable education experiences of my career.

## Key Takeaways:

- Broker support matters. Align yourself with a brokerage that actively educates its licensees and backs them through complex challenges.

- Education is your armor. Take full advantage of every training session, workshop, and affiliate presentation your brokerage offers.

- Never skip due diligence. Even if your client feels confident, ensure there's ample time for research, surveys, and potential red flags.

- Always recommend property surveys. Knowing where the lines *really* are, can save your client from major headaches (and you from liability).

- Persistence pays off. A successful outcome may take time, effort, and grit, but the lessons are often worth far more than the commission.

Notes: _____

# The Grow Operation

It was a modest, unassuming home, nothing flashy, just a typical property recently vacated by a tenant. The seller had accepted an offer, and as was customary, a home inspection was scheduled. The buyer met the inspector at the house to walk through together, an experience meant to provide peace of mind and reassurance about the home's condition.

Room by room, the inspection proceeded with the usual banter and notes. But then they reached the basement.

When the light switch was flipped on, the scene that unfolded caught both men off guard. Rows of benches lined one wall, dotted with planting pots still filled with soil. Gardening tools hung neatly nearby, and large overhead grow lights loomed above the benches like silent sentinels. It looked... odd.

That's when the inspector made a flippant comment: "Looks like a grow operation."

The moment the words left his mouth, the tone of the showing changed. The buyer stiffened, took one more look around, and abruptly left the property. To him, the suggestion, whether serious or not, was enough to shatter the image of the wholesome, family home he'd hoped for. Marijuana was still illegal at the time, and the idea that it might have been grown in the basement where he planned to raise children was a dealbreaker.

Just like that, the transaction died.

Later, as the agents unpacked what had gone wrong, they learned the full truth. The previous tenant was a little old lady who grew African violets, delicate flowers that thrive under specific lighting conditions and require a balance of light and dark to flourish. She had supplied blooms to local flower shops for years. The lights, the benches, the pots, it all made perfect sense.

But the damage was done.

This is a lesson that cuts deep in our profession: careless words, especially during inspections or showings, can have irreversible consequences. In this case, a casual comment, spoken without intent to harm, cost the seller a deal and the buyer a home.

# Key Takeaways: Inspections & African Violets

- Inspectors should inspect, not influence. A professional home inspector's role is to identify defects or concerns, not speculate or editorialize. Their words carry significant weight and can derail a transaction if carelessly delivered.

- Buyers rely on tone as much as content. An inspector's demeanor and delivery can reinforce, or completely reverse, a buyer's emotional connection to a home. Comments that go beyond the facts can breed unnecessary fear, doubt, or offense.

- Facts, not assumptions. Jumping to conclusions based on appearances (e.g., grow lights and benches = illegal activity) without context or confirmation can create irreversible damage to a deal.

- Vetting inspectors matters. Real estate professionals should recommend inspectors who not only have technical expertise but also a strong sense of professionalism, discretion, and respect for the buyer-seller dynamic.

- Defuse with preparation. Whenever possible, prepare your clients for what to expect during inspections. Let them know inspectors are not decorators, appraisers, or therapists, and sometimes their delivery can come off a little… unfiltered.

Notes:_____
_____
_____
_____
_____
_____
_____
_____

# Reflection & Discussion

1. What's the most unexpected challenge you've ever faced right before closing?
   How did you handle it, and would you do anything differently now?

2. Have you ever misunderstood (or overlooked) a key clause in a contract?
   What did you learn from that experience?

3. Do you have a consistent way to double-check terms, numbers, and conditions before presenting or accepting offers?
   What's your process?

4. Think about a time when a deal *almost* fell apart.
   What saved it, and what caused the issue in the first place?

5. How do you keep your attention sharp when you're overwhelmed, distracted, or just plain tired?

6. What tools or habits help you avoid mistakes under pressure?

Notes: _____
_____
_____
_____
_____
_____
_____
_____
_____

# Chapter Four

## Service, Standards & Showing Up - *The Job Isn't Over When the Deal Closes*

Great service doesn't come from memorizing the contract or quoting market stats. It comes from showing up , when it's inconvenient, when it's messy, and when nobody's watching. These are the moments your clients remember: when you cleaned a house yourself, gave up a holiday, or stepped in after another licensee dropped the ball.

This section is a tribute to what it really means to serve. Not perform, not posture , but *serve*. Sometimes it looks like heroics, but more often, it's about consistency, empathy, and doing what's right even when no one would've blamed you for walking away.

Because professionalism isn't just what you *say* you'll do. It's what you actually do , again and again , when it matters most.

# Three Curveballs and a White Picket Fence

In the earlier days of my career, before smartphones and FaceTime tours, I worked with a relocating buyer who was an Air Force officer and dentist transferring to Elmendorf Air Force Base in Anchorage. We'd been communicating long-distance for weeks, reviewing listings and planning a full itinerary of properties to tour in the Valley until the night before his arrival when I got Curveball #1.

"I didn't realize I have to live within 20 minutes of the base hospital," he said. "I can't live in the Valley."

My heart sank. All that work was gone. I offered to refer him to a licensee in Anchorage, but Curveball #2 was right behind it.

"I don't want anyone else," he said. "I want to work with you."

Anchorage wasn't my typical market at the time. Scheduling showings was labor-intensive, as I didn't even have access to their lockboxes. But I couldn't say no. His loyalty inspired my own. I made it happen, with help from colleagues and late nights reworking schedules after full days of showings.

We spent the next few days searching Anchorage, then expanding outward into Eagle River, Chugiak, and Peters Creek. And that's when Curveball #3 hit, in the form of a charming yellow two-story home with a white picket fence and a For Sale By Owner sign out front.

The seller greeted us from his grill on the front porch. "I'll show it to you," he said. "But I'm not paying a commission."

Without skipping a beat, my client looked the seller in the eye and said, "Don't worry about her commission. I'll pay it."

I was stunned. No buyer had ever offered that before. This was before buyer representation agreements were common practice. But this client knew my value, maybe more than I did at the time.

He bought the home, paid my brokerage fee, and reminded me that loyalty, service, and professionalism don't go unnoticed. And sometimes, they come back to you in the most unexpected and heartwarming ways.

## Key Takeaways :

Loyalty is earned through service, and when clients feel seen and supported, they respond in kind.

- The extra mile matters, especially when clients are navigating major life transitions.

- Working without a guaranteed commission doesn't mean working without value. True professionalism often comes full circle.

- The FSBOs may hold surprises. Never discount an opportunity because it doesn't fit the usual mold.

- In a world where buyer agreements are now standard, this story reminds us why they became necessary, and why relationships are still the foundation of real estate.

Notes: _____

_____
_____
_____
_____
_____
_____
_____
_____
_____
_____
_____

# Signed But Not Delivered

In the ever-evolving world of real estate, the rise of team structures and buyer representation agreements brought both clarity and complications. One of my newer licensees at that time, still learning the ropes but already sharp and intuitive, came to me with an issue that struck at the core of professionalism and service.

He had just taken a call from a tearful woman who, along with her husband, had been relocated to Alaska by his employer. They were desperately trying to secure a home before the move. They'd already lost out on several homes and were under immense pressure, both logistically and emotionally. The buyer asked if she was under any kind of agreement with another brokerage, and she answered with a clear "no." Confident he could help, my licensee sprang into action.

He drove to a completed new construction listing that fit their criteria, did a FaceTime showing with the buyer, and they quickly submitted an offer, which was accepted.

A few days later, however, the storm rolled in. A team lead from another brokerage called and insisted they were entitled to the commission because the buyers had signed a representation agreement. My licensee came to me immediately. I contacted the couple and discovered the truth: the wife wasn't aware her husband had signed a buyer agreement. When asked why they didn't continue working with that team, their answer revealed a troubling lack of service and foresight.

They'd flown to Alaska for a whirlwind home-buying weekend, fully expecting their agent to be prepared and available. Instead, the team member showed up late to their first showing with no urgency or respect for their tight schedule. After showing just a couple of homes, she casually told them she'd see them again on Sunday, completely disregarding their limited availability.

When they pressed about Saturday showings, she explained the entire team was attending a wedding and no one was available. The couple was left to drive around alone, peeking at listings from their rental car, wasting time and money. On Sunday, she showed them a few more homes, and they finally identified one to make an offer on, only to be told she'd write the offer the next day. By the time she submitted it on Tuesday, the property was already under contract with another buyer.

Heartbroken and frustrated, they moved on and connected with my licensee, who did everything right. He understood their urgency and made them a priority.

After speaking with the other agent and her broker, I laid the facts on the table. I didn't sugarcoat anything. Her team had failed these clients. They missed every opportunity to serve and support them. My licensee, on the other hand, had gone above and beyond, even offering to forfeit his commission in order to represent them properly.

In the end, I negotiated a 10% consolation fee to the other brokerage in exchange for not pursuing a claim against the buyers. It was a small price to pay for preserving the integrity of the transaction and protecting clients who had been so poorly treated.

# Key Takeaways

- A buyer representation agreement is only as strong as the service provided behind it. Contracts don't ensure loyalty, relationships do.

- It's essential to ask *both* buyers if they've signed any agreements before moving forward, especially when only one is actively involved in communication.

- The best agents prioritize their clients' needs over convenience or commission.

- Strong broker support and ethical leadership can resolve tough situations before they escalate.

Notes:

# When the Cost Is Too High

There's a perception that real estate professionals set their own hours. And while that's technically true, what many outside the industry don't understand is that those hours are often dictated by the needs and schedules of clients, not the licensee. Especially in the early years of building a business, boundaries can blur in the pursuit of closing deals and proving your worth.

In those early days of my career, I was a single mother, newly divorced and determined to make real estate work. My two boys were young, and we shared a week-on, week-off custody schedule with their dad. Thanksgiving was one of those "on" days, it was my turn to have them.

But that Thanksgiving, I also had out-of-town buyers in town for the holiday weekend. They were eager to find a home during their time off and wanted to see a property, that day. And back then, before buyer-broker agreements were common, there were no guarantees a client would stay loyal to the licensee who showed them homes. I had already invested time into these buyers and didn't want to risk losing the sale.

I promised my boys it would only take an hour.

That hour turned into two. Then three. One more showing. One more drive-by. And by the time I got home, it was just in time to give my boys a quick hug and send them out the door with their father.

I missed Thanksgiving with them.

To make matters worse, the buyers ended up making an offer, on that first home I showed them, but the offer was so low, the sellers were insulted and refused to respond. The sale never happened. And the moment with my boys was gone forever.

To this day, that decision haunts me.

Even now, as seasoned as I am, I can't tell that story without my voice catching. My boys are in their 40s now with kids of their own. We're still close, but that day taught me a lesson I've carried through my entire career: no commission is worth missing out on the moments that matter most.

Key Takeaways :

- Boundaries matter. Clients will take as much of you as you allow. Set limits early and protect the people and priorities that matter most.

- Don't confuse hustle with success. Being constantly available doesn't make you more professional, it can erode your well-being and relationships.

- Regret lingers longer than opportunity. Deals fall apart all the time. But time with your family is priceless, and once it's gone, you can't get it back.

- Real estate is about service, but not self-sacrifice. You can give your best to your clients without giving them *all* of you.

Notes: _____

# Ethical Dilemma

Recently, two of my licensees came to me with a tough situation, one of those moments where professional lines get blurry, emotions get high, and ethics take center stage.

They were representing a buyer who had negotiated a solid deal on a new home. Everything was progressing smoothly, until the appraisal came in. And it came in low. *Tens of thousands of dollars low.* Suddenly, the deal was in jeopardy. The listing licensee, trying to salvage the transaction, reached out to the lender to explore options for bridging the gap.

And that's where things went sideways.

The lender, whether out of carelessness, inexperience, or just plain ignorance, told the listing licensee that the buyer "had plenty of money" to make up the difference. A serious breach of confidentiality. But what happened next was even more complicated.

The listing licensee then told my licensees what the lender had said. "In confidence."

And just like that, everyone was tangled up in an ethical mess. To make this even more complicated, the buyer, seller, & lender knew each other on a personal level, and my licensees didn't want to put a damper on their relationship. My licensees didn't know what to do. On one hand, they had a duty to their buyer. On the other, they didn't want to damage their working relationship with the listing licensee. They were caught between professionalism and allegiance, ethics and etiquette. They asked me for guidance.

I told them this: *Your duty is to your client. Period.* It's not their decision on whether this information will be harmful to the buyer's relationships, especially when that information has the potential to financially harm your client. If the buyer were to agree to a counteroffer above the appraised value, without knowing the full picture, that would be a clear violation of our duty to advocate and protect their best interest.

The lender's statement created an unfair disadvantage for the buyer. By sharing confidential information with the seller's side, he compromised the entire negotiation dynamic. And now that information exists, it cannot be ignored. In the end, I reminded my licensees that if standing up for what's right may not be convenient, it is always essential. The buyer deserved the truth, even if it meant discomfort for the professionals involved.

☙

## Key Takeaways :

- Confidentiality is non-negotiable. Lenders must protect their clients' private financial data. Breaches like this erode trust and violate federal lending laws and ethical principles.

- Fiduciary duty outweighs professional courtesy. Our primary obligation is to the client, not to another licensee's ego or reputation.

- Once you know, you can't unknow. If information impacts your client's decision-making, you have a duty to act on it, even if it was shared "in confidence."

- Advocacy means discomfort sometimes. Ethical representation often requires hard conversations and firm boundaries.

Notes: _____

_____
_____
_____
_____
_____
_____
_____
_____
_____
_____
_____
_____
_____

## *Reflection & Discussion*

1. When have you had to "show up" in a situation you wanted to walk away from?
   What made you stay?

2. How do you define professionalism , not just in appearance, but in action?
   How has that definition changed over the years?

3. Have you ever had to advocate for a client when it meant risking a relationship with another licensee or affiliate?
   What did you learn?

4. Where do you draw the line between keeping the peace and doing what's right?
   How do you handle that tension?

5. Who's someone you've worked with that exemplified both heart and high standards?

6. What can you learn from them?

Notes: _____

_____
_____
_____
_____
_____
_____
_____
_____
_____
_____
_____
_____
_____
_____
_____

# Chapter Five

## Beans, Burn Barrels, and Barney

Some stories stick with you not because of the transaction, but because of the people. Ron and Pam were among the first clients I ever worked with, and to this day, they remain two of my all-time favorites. Over the course of 30 years, I've represented them on more than a dozen properties. But there's one property in particular that continues to make us laugh, a home tucked off Knik River Road with a view of the Chugach Range and just enough quirks to make it memorable.

Pam, Ron, and I had been out looking at properties one afternoon, feeling a little punchy after a long day of showings. When we pulled into the driveway of this one, the first thing we saw was a concrete block foundation, about four blocks high, and standing inside of it, a beautiful horse. Not tied up nearby. Not standing outside the structure. No, this horse was inside the foundation, as if waiting for us to marvel at its placement.

We weren't sure how it got in there or how anyone expected it to get out, but the sight struck Pam and me as absolutely hilarious. We laughed until we couldn't breathe. Pam started snorting, which set me off even more. Poor Ron just stood by, shaking his head and letting us have our moment.

Despite the horse, they loved the house. It needed some cleanup and a few updates, like new carpeting, but it had potential. Since Ron and Pam lived in Southeast Alaska, I offered to gift them the cleanup work as a closing gift. My teenage son Scooter and one of his friends were enlisted to help clear the yard and pull up the carpet.

We arrived early that morning with trash bags, gloves, and a can-do attitude. I had the boys working in the yard while I went inside to clean. The light fixtures were dusty and full of cobwebs, so I removed the glass covers and decided to run them through the dishwasher. There was no dishwasher detergent, but I found a bottle of dish soap and figured that would do. Spoiler alert: it would not.

As I was finishing up loading the dishwasher, the boys came inside to ask if they could burn some of the trash in a barrel out back. I gave the standard mom warning: "Be careful." Then I went back to my cleaning.

Suddenly, I heard loud popping sounds from outside. Curious (and maybe a little concerned), I stepped out the back door. The boys had a fire blazing in the burn barrel, and the popping was from aerosol cans they'd tossed in, spray paint, hairspray, who knows what else. I was just about to scold them when a massive BOOM echoed through the yard.

Beans. It was raining baked beans.

Unbeknownst to me, they'd thrown a family-size can of baked beans into the barrel, and it chose that moment to explode. The three of us scattered, ducking for cover. Meanwhile, my sidekick, a chubby little dachshund named Barney, took full advantage of the chaos, gobbling up every bean he could find.

After collecting myself and getting Barney under control, I headed back inside to check on the dishwasher. I opened the door to the kitchen and froze. The floor was covered, knee-deep in suds. Turns out, regular dish soap in a dishwasher creates a never-ending supply of bubbles. Bubbles everywhere. They were pouring out of the machine like something out of a sitcom.

Despite the explosions, the beans, and the bubble tsunami, we got the place cleaned up. Ron and Pam were thrilled with the house, and that wild day became one of our favorite shared memories. Every time we reconnect, that story comes up, followed by a round of laughter that rivals our first.

The lesson? Real estate is more than just contracts and closing dates. It's about relationships. It's about showing up, even after the ink is dry, and making sure your clients are cared for. It's about creating stories that will be told for decades. And sometimes, it's about ducking exploding beans and chasing down a dachshund named Barney.

# Acknowledgments

There are far too many people to name who have influenced my career, my decisions, and this book, but there are a few I simply can't move forward without recognizing.

**Kevin Crozier**

If you ask me to name just one person who has shaped my real estate moral compass, it's Kevin. I'm not sure he even knows the impact he's had on me. Kevin was licensed a few years before I was, and he quickly became one of the most successful, and most grounded licensees this community has ever known.

He's always been honest, fair, and quietly wise. In fact, one of the most grounding pieces of advice I've ever received came from him during a tough situation. After listening carefully, he paused, and asked me: *"What are you pretending not to know?"* That question stopped me in my tracks, and it's stayed with me ever since. Kevin now works under my license and runs his own branch office, but I'll always see him as one of my most important mentors.

**Tammy Hansen**

Tammy has been one of those rare people who shows up with a smile, offers encouragement without asking for anything in return, and makes everything feel lighter just by being there. She made one of my birthdays the most memorable I've ever had as an adult, and not just because we were in Las Vegas.

Let's just say that if you've ever walked a long hallway flanked by hundreds of people who seem *far too interested* in your arrival... you start to wonder. We later found out that we were unintentionally part of the entrance parade for a group of adult film stars heading into a major industry event. So yes, here's to walking with the porn stars, Tammy. And thank you for walking with *me* in all the ways that really matter.

## Krystal Rogers

There's no one else I could've built this next chapter of my career with. When Krystal and I joined forces, we didn't start from scratch. She had already built the foundation of Elite Real Estate Group, navigating her way through two previous partnerships. I had my own brokerage, and she had been my licensee in years past. When the time was right, we brought our strengths together and merged our companies. I was letting go of the RE/MAX brand, and keeping the Elite name just made sense - financially, practically, and culturally. Thankfully, my licensees agreed.

We started with about 35 people. Today, just a few short years later, we've grown to over 65 , and that has everything to do with what Krystal brings to the table. She is the heart of our company culture. She's fun, warm, and completely committed to making every person in our brokerage feel seen, valued, and loved. She's good at all the things I'm not, and maybe that's why it works.

Krystal will tell you I'm the contract nerd, the one who handles the legal, the structure, the risk management. And she's not wrong. I'm the strict mom. She's the fun aunt. Together, we've built something I'm incredibly proud of. Thank you, Krystal, for being the kind of partner who makes business better, and makes people better, too.

## Jessica Frank

Some acknowledgments are easy. Others are complicated. Not because there isn't love, but because there's *so much of it*, layered with history, family ties, and emotions that don't fit neatly into paragraphs. Jessica is all of that and more.

She's been part of my life since she and my son Travis were teenagers. Long before real estate ever paid the bills, she was around the house, and I, brand new to the industry, put her to work the old-school way, cutting and pasting actual photos onto actual paper flyers. Glue sticks and property sheets. That's where it started. She physically filed the carbon copies of my contracts.

Since then, she's been in and out of real estate. Jessica has held nearly every role imaginable: unlicensed assistant, bookkeeper, licensed transaction coordinator, new licensee trainer, office manager, and our company's code compliance officer. She's been my right hand through some of the most demanding seasons of my career.

She's also the mother of four of my grandchildren. I love her as fiercely as if she were my own daughter. And like many in-law relationships, ours comes with its fair share of complexity. We've had moments, ones where I've held my breath, bit my tongue, or blinked back tears for the sake of peace and family. I'm sure she's done the same. That's the truth. That's me and Jess.

But through every twist and turn, she's shown up. She's worked hard. She's carried responsibilities most people never even see; but I see them. I see *her*. And I'm so grateful for all the ways she's been a part of my career.

**To the licensees I've mentored...**
Thank you for trusting me to guide you, whether for a season or a career. You challenged me, inspired me, and reminded me every day why this work matters.

**To the staff and affiliate partners who keep everything moving...**
From title and escrow to lenders, inspectors, and office managers, thank you for being the behind-the-scenes heroes who make impossible timelines, client meltdowns, and mountains of paperwork somehow manageable.

**To my fellow brokers and instructors...**
It's been an honor to teach, learn, collaborate, and grow beside you. Thank you for pushing the standards higher, holding the line on ethics, and sharing the kind of wisdom that only comes from being *in it*.

**To my students...**
You've sat through my stories, laughed at the wild ones, and hopefully took something useful with you into the field. Thank you for showing up eager to learn, and for making this next generation of professionals, one I'm proud to pass the torch to.

**To my Elite Real Estate Group family...**
Every single one of you has helped shape this company, this book, and this journey. Thank you for showing up, stepping up, and making this a team to be proud of.

*It's time to fly the plane....*

TjB

Made in the USA
Columbia, SC
17 June 2025